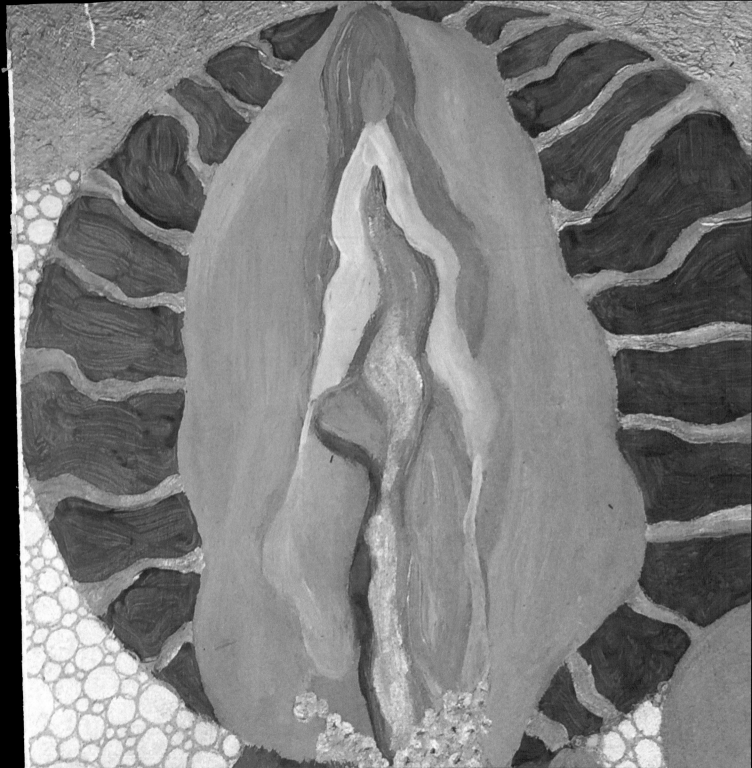

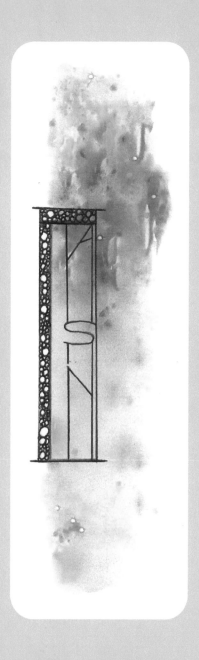

Published by:

Fumbled Book Press
Oakland, CA

Second Edition 2021 Jan

inherimage@artlover.com
www.inherimagestudio.com
San Francisco, California USA

ISBN: 978-0-9987640-3-0

Joan and David Lincer, Publishers

Fumbled Book Press brings titles that we know and love back from "Out of Print". Each title is reset with care using Adobe InDesign.

Catalog at: www.FumbledBookPress.com

SOFT POWER
RECLAIMING THE SACRED CUNT PROJECT

DEBORAH K. TASH
WHITE WOLF WOMAN

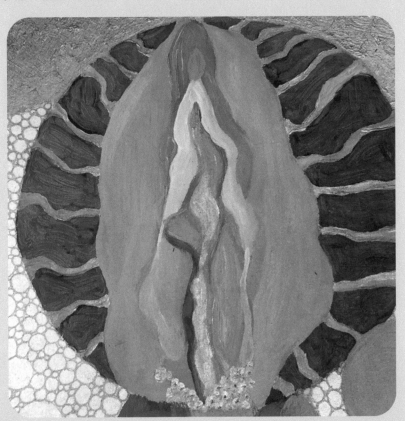

Dedication

For all the women who have endured sexual trauma; sexual abuse, molestation, physical abuse and survived to heal and reclaim their lives and power.

For all the women who have struggled to embrace their beauty and sacred sexuality, doing so regardless of pain and censure.

For all the women who have not yet found their voices and been able to tell their stories. May they find the courage and strength to do so.

In gratitude for the elder pioneers who have paved the way for the current understanding and solidarity of the #metoo movement by telling their stories, making their art, sharing their strength and dedication with courage and love.

For each and every woman as the embodiment of the Divine Feminine on earth and all those men who cherish them, connecting with their inner Divine Feminine and acting as allies...

With special thanks to Audrey D. Cole and Frederick V. Cook

TABLE OF CONTENTS

vi

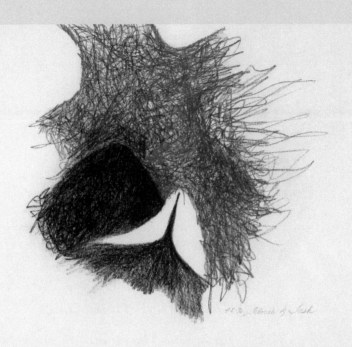

Introduction

Cunt

[kuhnt]

All senses of this word are considered vulgar slang and are very strongly tabooed and censored. The meanings that refer to a woman and a contemptible person interchangeably are used with disparaging intent and are perceived as highly insulting and demeaning. There are many words used to refer to people in sexual terms. However, to call a person a cunt, especially a woman, is one of the most hateful and powerful examples of verbal abuse in the English language.

In these times of patriarchal polarization, hatred of women's power is rampant worldwide even though there is a renewed understanding of the Divine Feminine and women's profound influence. The word cunt continues to have a pejorative meaning. Some in current cultures have taken to using the word very casually. Men call men they intend to denigrate cunts, coupling feminine qualities to the word implying that the man is worthless, weak and useless because he has womanly characteristics, even more insidious than calling him a pussy, another slang word for female genitalia! Even young women refer to women and men they don't like or respect as cunts, both denigrating themselves with internalized sexism and devaluing the power of women.

The question that keeps coming up for me as an artist is; how is it that the images of cunt which are evident in nature taboo? I see them in trees, in caverns, in the entrances to caves and underground tunnels. They are in plants, rock formations and, of course, in female animals and humans. Look at tree trunks, into the center of a rose or the mouth of a cave, the image of cunt is everywhere in nature.

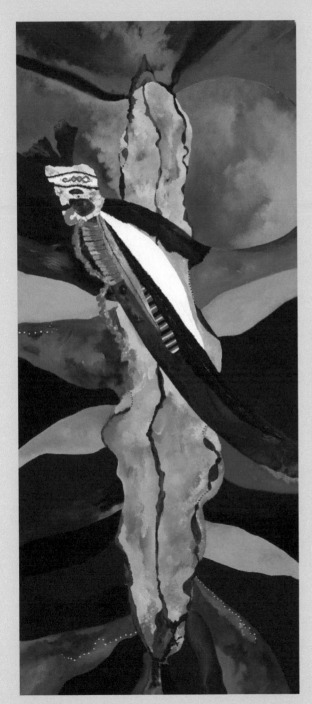

But, of course, it isn't only the images that are considered a problem, something to be ashamed of; profane and vulgar. It's the word, cunt. If used to describe a woman it connotes a woman who is misbehaving, unmanageable, independent, and opinionated. She thinks for herself, is wild, and untamed. Not unlike nature.

Just stand up for yourself against a male who is steeped in patriarchal social conditioning and see how quickly you are called a cunt. This kind of woman isn't obedient, submissive or docile. She may not have much respect for social norms which relegate her to second class citizenry or expect her to obey and concede to male ego and domination. She is most likely ambitious and may be quite competitive, making her own choices and way in the world. She doesn't conform. She's "selfish". She's the opposite of the passive, docile, self-sacrificing, people-pleasing mother archetype which is the main socially approved role allowed to women, even now in the 21st Century!

This woman is more in tune with the warrior-goddess, High Priestess, leader and huntress archetypes and she isn't particularly interested in being passive-aggressive, either. Most probably when one is using the term cunt in a derogatory manner, the woman in question is being characterized as rude, overbearing and abrasive when, in fact, she may simply be direct, speaking her truth and being true to herself in the same way that men are rewarded for culturally.

I acknowledge that there are many unstable and unbalanced women who are manipulative and vindictive, cause heartache and suffering for those around them and are in need of professional assistance in order to find a more positive and fulfilling way in the world. An overwhelming number of these strong willed women are difficult because of sexual abuse trauma (often repressed to protect themselves) as children or adults, as well as physical abuse at the hands of men. Cultures that enable patriarchal mistreatment of women both physically and emotionally, curtailing their freedom and ability to be the best of themselves create the conditions that lead to that kind of twisted self-protective behavior. Still, they do not deserve to be called pejorative names that belittle them simply because they are women! They are attempting to assert themselves, albeit in a destructive manner, in a culture that has consistently devalued them.

The Soft Power Series became Soft Power/ Reclaiming The Sacred Cunt Project to include the Shamanic aspect of my art, as well as the activist aspect. Shamanism as a practice for reaching altered states of consciousness by inducing trance during ritual has deep roots in many cultures. The Shaman invokes the powers of the spirit world and elementals, connecting to ancient and transformational energies, as do magicians, witches, sorcerers and all those who tap into what is currently being called the Quantum Field. It is the power of intention that directs the energy of the Quantum Field for desired results.

Art and ritual are intertwined. Inducing trance states for creating art is a Shamanic act; the two have been woven together for millennia to create change, heal trauma, disease and physical injuries. When ancient peoples drew images of animals on cave walls to connect with their spirits, they were channeling these energies for healing, spiritual evolution and creativity, seeking connection with their primal power.

The artist and poet as Shaman, dedicated to the Sacred Feminine, acts as a conduit, allowing the spirit of the Divine Feminine, the Goddess in her many guises, access during the creation of art. Channeling the Muse is another way to think of the experience of trance and art making which allows access to both spirit energies and to parts of the self and Self. Some call on the elementals; spirits of earth, air, fire and water, as well as totem animals and guides. Any and all are available and this access channeled into the creation of art and poetry makes them available for community, to facilitate healing, to inspire, give solace and share blessings.

...

I began to explore images of cunt and sexuality as an art student in the 1970s and when I saw Judy Chicago's Dinner Party in the early 1980s I was profoundly affected both as an artist and as a sexual abuse survivor. Focused through the lens of my Wiccan practice, the Dinner Party gave my own work renewed perspective. My commitment to wholeness and balanced mental health challenged me to be receptive to the beauty and inspiration of this groundbreaking work. Knowing that cunt is a sacred word evocative of the Divine Feminine in every woman, my exploration as an artist deepened.

Initially triggered by the exhibit I found myself intent upon increasing understanding about my own background, as well as exploring how to heal myself through my art. My childhood was marked by sexual and physical abuse at the hands of my grandfather at age three who attempted to kill me when I refused his continued sexual molestation and into my teen years with my stepfather's physical abuse and sexual molestation. Being a survivor became the central issue for me as I grew up in a household of violence and profound neglect. After many years of therapy and healing practices I reached a point of stability which allowed me to take a deeper dive into healing through art.

Over the ensuing years I have shown the project as it has evolved in several venues since its inception in the mid-1980s, most recently in late 2019 in the ARISE GALLERY in San Francisco, California and been gratified at the supportive and positive response that it has received. Recently after reading Eve Ensler's newest book, The Apology, I realized that Soft Power/ Reclaiming The Sacred Cunt Project needed to include more than my art and poetry, but also my story. I have included some very personal poems and stories in this book to that end.

Creating images and objects both with mixed media, ceramics, and paint, as well as with the power of words via poetry, Soft Power/Reclaiming The Sacred Cunt Project is dedicated to exploring female sexual power to heal and alchemize trauma through the creation of beautiful and potent art. Informed by the practice of Shamanism, Tantra, Goddess worship and the influence of the Divine Feminine. I offer you these rich images as photographs and poems. Recognizing in nature the evocative opening for spiritual sexuality which every woman possesses as an integral part of her being I reclaim both the word cunt and the images of cunt we find ourselves surrounded by everywhere in the world; for myself, and for you.

Deborah K. Tash
April 2020
San Francisco, CA

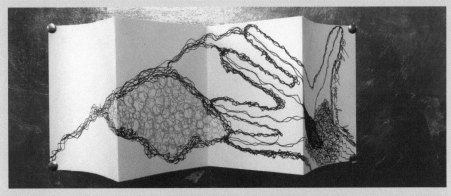

Cunt Questions

It's time to reclaim the word cunt and the power that it implies!
Here are some questions to stimulate discussion and consideration:

- **What do you think of the role of the artist as shaman and activist for social change; the artist as boundary pusher and shit disturber?**

- **What is your relationship to your sexuality with your spirituality? Do you know about Tantra?**

- **How do you see female sexuality in conjunction with spirituality in terms of society?**

- **How do you feel about the way the word cunt is used as a pejorative, as taboo and derogatory? Are you willing to change your mind about the word and reclaim it for yourself?**

- **Have you noticed cunt images in nature and how do you feel about them? Do you see them as evidence of the beauty of the Goddess in all of life?**

- **Have you considered that your sexuality is a source of your power? If so, how does that show up in your life?**

2

Reclaiming The Sacred Cunt

A Brief Essay For Completing The Circle: Rape and Female Genital Mutilation:

Lately I have been reading articles written about the young women who were sexually assaulted and raped by Jeffrey Epstein and his associates. One in a recent issue of Vanity Fair was especially well written and provocative. The accounts detailed the experiences of the young women when most of them were underage, as young as fourteen. With only a few exceptions these vulnerable young girls were taken advantage of by older men in positions of power and wealth. Often one of the main questions when details are written and reported about these women and girl's experiences is "Why didn't the girls and women say 'no' and put a stop to the rape and abuse?" or " Why didn't they go to the police and report the incident?"

The collusion of Ghislaine Maxwell who acted as procuress for Epstein and his cronies, notwithstanding, the answer lies in the imbalance of power between the men and the young girls. (Not to mention the humiliation and mistreatment regularly experienced at the hands of 'helpful authorities' who are also mostly men.) Men who held the promise of money and beneficial positions as bait for economically disadvantaged young girls were also leveraging their power against them. Having been sexually assaulted and raped myself as a young woman, I am reminded of the maelstrom of emotions that is stirred up when a man overpowers with physical strength. The societal programming of a culture of rape that women receive to be malleable, cooperative and submissive to the will of men is a toxic confusion that interferes with a woman's need for self-protection. When you add in the underlying self-hatred and shame for their own sexuality and genitals most women experience, it becomes sadly understandable why many did not stand up for themselves or report the abuse afterwards.

Rape is a power dynamic played out in sexual terms. Sexual desire is subverted by the desire for domination, control and subversion of women's power. Patriarchal fear of women's power and sexuality reinforces women's distrust and disgust at their own sexuality because of centuries of brutalization, disempowerment and humiliation. Perpetrated by male domination this has led to a continually seething wound in the feminine psyche; an inability to say "NO, this is MY BODY!" which further emboldens males to rape, continuing the rape culture into the present time...2020!

Certainly there are many males who would

be undeterred by a strong woman's refusal to submit, especially in wartime where soldiers regularly use rape as a weapon. However, a woman's choice to stand up for herself, even if unable to put a stop to the assault or rape, contributes to her increased self-esteem. In the recent accounts of survivors who have finally been able to tell their stories, it is a welcome theme that runs through them.

The constant fear of being brutalized, sexually assaulted and raped has plagued women for milennia leaving them fearful of going out alone at night and saying "no" to men's sexual demands, among other fears of men. The internalization of these fears has also led to internalized sexism and women's hatred of their own genitalia and sexuality.

It would seem that in 2020 such issues would already be addressed and handled. The #metoo movement has definitely made inroads, affording a new sense of feminine empowerment. When enough women stand up and refuse to be assaulted, fighting back, it shifts the imbalance of power dynamic. But there is still more work to do. Female genital mutilation continues in Africa, the Middle East and in over half the countries of the world, spread by migration and culture from one country to another; often performed on kitchen tables. Rape is regularly used as a weapon in wars to demoralize the population. The process of

conquest, domestication, and enslavement is a very old one, and it persists in modern times. The threat of violence remains in the present, it is not overtly needed if the subjugated person obeys and does not question the "superior authority", withhold expected services, or otherwise rebel. And the use of the word cunt as a pejorative continues. Dehumanizing name-calling is a threat and clear step in the cycle of violent abuse.

Women are also carriers of culture. Female genital mutilation is the ultimate form of rape and degradation of the sacred cunt. In some societies where it is practiced, the cutting off of the clitoris is only the beginning. The cutting off of all structures of the cunt, starting with the clitoris, includes cutting off the labia and then sewing up the entire area leaving only a small opening for menstruation and urination. This horror is perpetrated on girl babies, children and preteens. In cultures where female genital mutilation is passed from generation to generation, women are regularly the perpetrators on their own daughters; a practice of brutality disguised as being for "their own good" and a generational legacy passed down from mother to daughter. There can be an unconscious "repetition compulsion" associated with unhealed trauma that drives mothers to reenact the violence. The idea that genitalia are dirty, ugly and shameful is a central theme and justification. They are told that a girl who does not have themselves ritually cleansed by removing their genitals will never be married or acceptable in the community. Often the result is death from sepsis and complications.

It is long past time to put an end to rape culture and female genital mutilation, unfortunately the process of societal change is a long hard road, but in addition to movement toward this end, there is also precedent of some important societal ideologies being changed within a few short generations. This brings hope to me. Because women are the carriers of culture, passing down ideas and beliefs that shape each new generation, I feel it is essential that I participate with my art by creating and showing beautiful images of the sacred cunt whenever and wherever I can adding my voice to inspire women to love their bodies and begin to heal and reshape our cultures, starting with my own. and hopefully worldwide, as well.

Deborah K. Tash
September 28, 2020
San Francisco, CA

No!

Unaware of my value I let myself be used
Passive because I loved sex and approval
Not knowing I had the right
To choose who shared my treasure
Before I knew how to say "no"

A hard won lesson over time
So many abusers tolerated
In my confusion and fear
Without understanding power
My sexuality obscured without "no"

The final confirmation
For my sacred cunt
My sacred pleasure
Is knowing it is MINE
And I alone say "yes" or "no"

I catch my upper lip between my teeth
Memories of how many times I was raped
'Til I learned the power of my own voice
How to mobilize my will
Take back the night with "no"

22SEP20

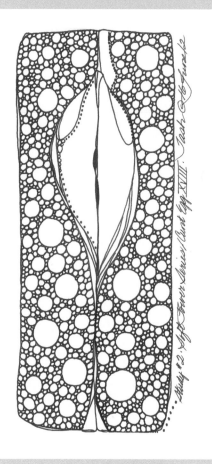

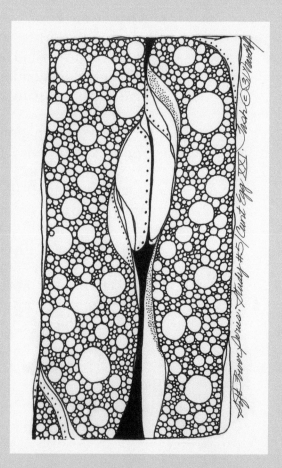

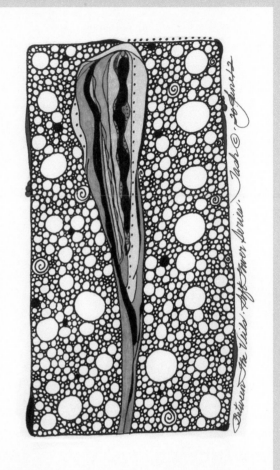

Between the Veils: Soft Inner Series. Trish © JoAnnetz

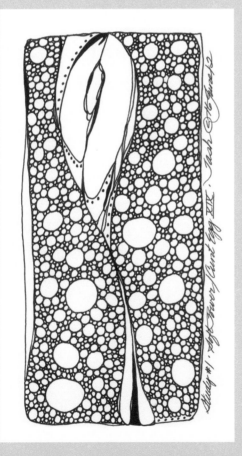

Study #1: Soft Inner/Cunt Egg IX. Trish © JoAnnetz

9

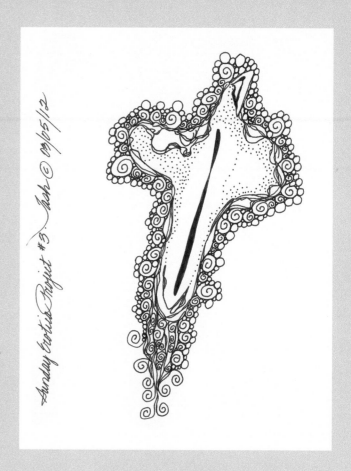

Sunday Erotica Project #3 Josh © 09/05/12

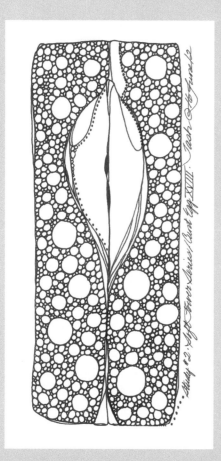

Study #3 Soft Paper Series Book 699 XVIII Josh © Groundz

10

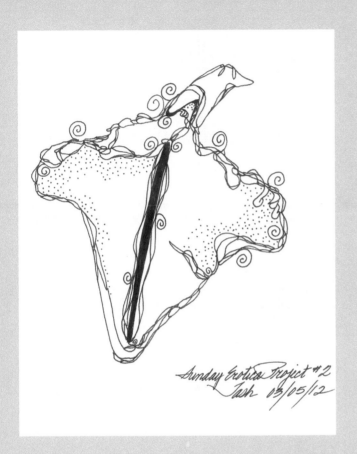

Sunday Erotica Project #2
Jash 03/05/12

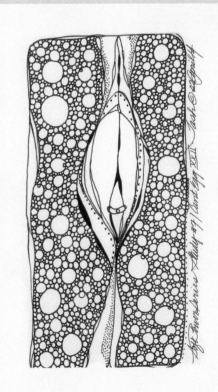

14

15

Shamanic Invocation I

Juicy
Ripe
Ready

Deepening truths wait
Centered in the Divine opening
The portal of pleasure
Of birth, rebirth, connection
Attendant on the spirits

Starting with convention
  vagina

Moving to playful
  pussy

To exotic Sanskrit
  yoni

Finally to taboo
  slit
  bush
  snatch

  cunt

I want to snatch it back
Raise my voice in praise
Invoking the powers of earth
Remind that sacred and profane
Are matters of perspective

28JUN14

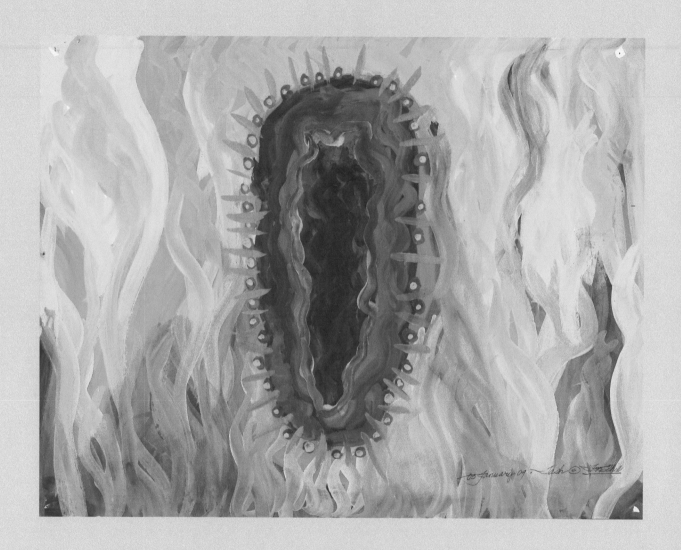

18

Speak to me

Let the flutter of wings
Write messages in the dew
Connecting me to morning

Speak to me

Let the voice of sunset
Whisper promises to my heart
Opening it for yearning

Speak to me

Let the ripples on a pond
Fill in the missing colors
Painting my eyes with wonder

Speak to me

Let the rush of waterfalls
Cleanse my anger and disbelief
Restoring my soul

Speak to me

Let your honeyed tongue
Open me to rapture
Celebrating each day in your honor

Speak to me

05JUL14

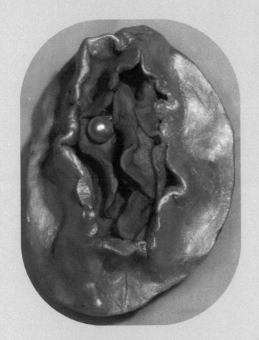

23

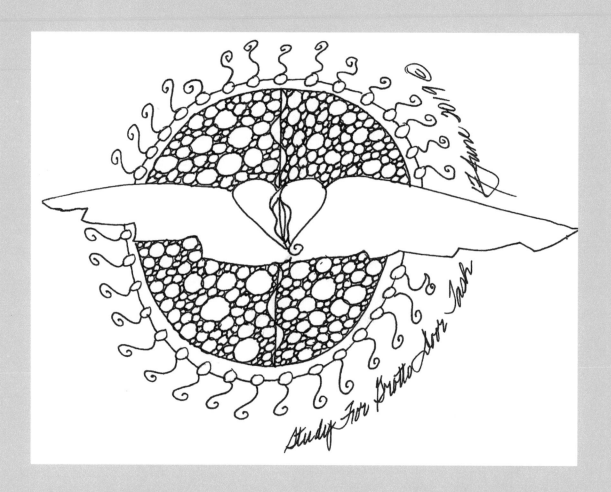

Shamanic Invocation II

Calling on the spirits of earth and air
Calling on the spirits of fire and water
Those first elementals in service of creation

Welcoming in the spirits of beauty
Those first to form the icons of Her grace
In every tree, waterfall and stone

Calling on the spirits of wind and mountain
Calling on the spirits of rain and flame
To set the table for Her feast

Welcoming Her sacred image
Found in the primal opening
Her desire before conception or birth

Calling on the spirits of shape and form
Calling on the spirits of dance and song
To manifest the soul of the eternal Goddess

Welcoming the knowledge of Her presence
In every portion of our bodies
Resonating in every cell with Her light

We call upon Her here
To bless us with Her primal soft power
And reclaim the sacred cunt in Her name

23JUL14

Invocation III

Let me be a voice
To praise your beauty
        your wisdom
        your desire

Let me be a drop
        in the ocean of your mystery
        your light
        your love

Let me be a hand
To paint your story
        your understanding
        your names

Let me be a channel
For your grace
        your face
        your voice

29AUG14

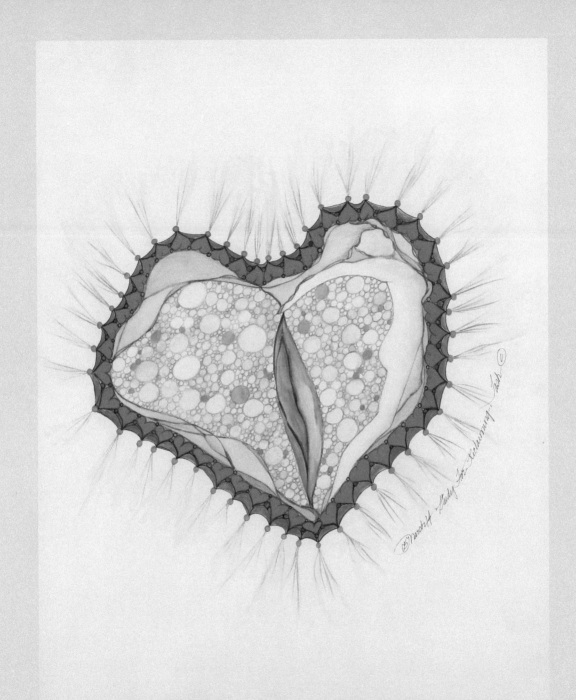

27

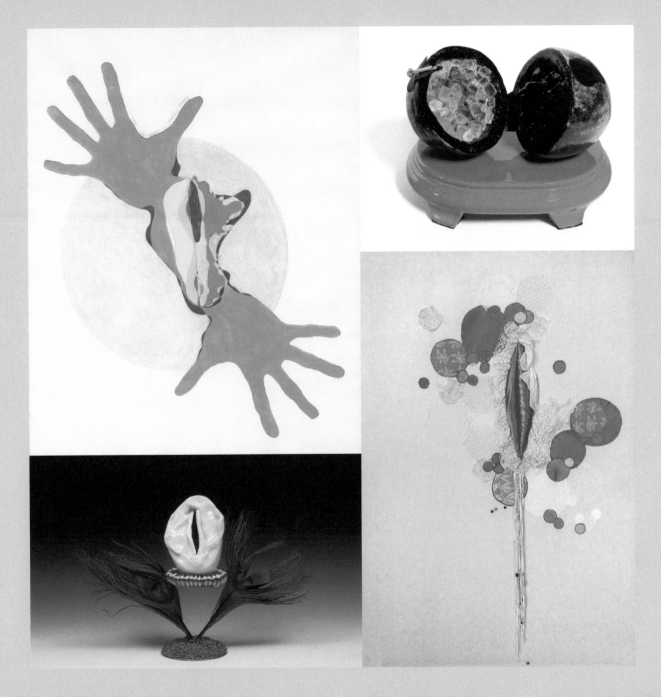

Where's That At?

I am constant in the darkness
A Northern Star
Lighting the way back from peril
With my own inner fire
Steady and stable
Even in the face of despair
A small twinkling beacon
At the end of a long slow tunnel

The Grandfather Chronicles

It was my grandfather's eyes and the sweetness of his presence that drew me into his orbit; that and my unrelenting child-need for connection. When the craziness was quiescent; the days when he wasn't lost in the distance of his depression, my grandfather was playful and fun. I was lonely and emotionally neglected with a pronounced limp undiagnosed as the results of polio. An emotionally distant father and a narcissistic self-absorbed mother, who did nothing about getting me medical care even though she had worked for years as a nurse, left me bereft and even more vulnerable than normal for a small child. It was his eyes and my loneliness and starvation for bonding that jeopardized my heart's freedom. It was his pain and mine that pulled me into the morass of my grandfather's stunted desire. I was two years old when it all began.

I'm not afraid of death, most times not my own, anyway. There is an edge that cuts deeply into the soul of mystery and captures the imagination when one tangos with death. It is an adult dance, not one meant for a child. Especially not for a child who collapses inward with the terror she believes is inherent in love. A child who lives within the closed walls of the past, preparing for annihilation. Such a one is not meant for the rigors of love equals death.

My constant and steadfast nature made a far too easy target in a family of the insane. My vulnerability and sensitivity guaranteed the hit. I am what is now referred to as A Highly Sensitive Person in pop psychology; because of my history? A sure thing for suffering, I didn't have the skills to dodge, be elusive or shrug off the hurt. What I did have was pride; pride that shielded me and sheltered me so that no one could get near enough to hurt me again. That last step, that no one was allowed to take, was the one I counted on as my protection. Now, finally, I write this down. At last, I write down the story of my grandfather's teachings on the annihilation of love.

It stood at the back of the yard, to the right of the garage, next to the ashen garbage can that my grandfather used to burn weeds and other waste from the garden. It was weathered and that kind of dark grey that old wood left unpainted becomes over the years of rain and sun and wind. It was also a dark vortex in my dreams. The work shed.

The dusty murky sunlight from a small window on the right side of the workbench was consumed by the shadowed interior. The rays of sunlight seemed to lose their direction as they passed through the spider webs and debris that obscured the graying glass, skittering around the room 'til they crashed on the floor and were eaten. In the middle of the shed was the old battered body of the Chevy. The old blackish Chevy, with its thorax and hooded malevolence, sat in the middle of the shed like a bloated black arachnid waiting patiently for its next victim. Its legs were tucked around it ready to spring. For the rest of my life, I would feel the shock of fear when I saw an old Chevy pickup of any color, anywhere. Eight legged crawlers sent me to the therapist seeking a way to diffuse the terror that any spider

elicited; a full-blown phobia.

Slowly I unravel this story; intent upon putting it down on paper in order to transform its power in my life from trauma to a reframing that serves my growth. So many memories fill the space between the pages.

My grandfather was a charmer, but his brother had spent most of his life in an insane asylum. All these years later I have learned that the disease that most likely twisted both his smile and his brother's life was called manic-depression. Here in the early 21st century, it is popularly named bi-polar disease. There are drugs and treatments for it in outpatient clinics and psychiatrists' offices outside of the insane asylums absent from our "modern" life.

Instead of asylums, the insane who cannot afford treatment sleep on street corners, piss in doorways and pollute the air of buses with their freshly shit-stained clothes, mumbling and cursing and yelling at the top of their lungs. How many of them are manic-depressive? I cringe sometimes just sitting down in a bus with the thought of who might have last sat in the seat. What might have been on their clothing leaving its residue? What infection from their lungs or bugs from their hair might they pass along? Will their crazy infect me? This is our legacy from a governor who also thought that when you'd seen one redwood, you'd seen them all. We no longer have places where such people can get "three squares and a cot" in relative safety in California. But I digress.

"Relative safety" is one of those terms with layers of meaning. Relatives, who are supposed to be safe, often are not. It took years of living with completely repressed memories before I found my way to the office of my first breakthrough therapist. My live-in lover at the time was seeing Ken on an irregular basis to explore his creative blocks. Ken was a therapist who specialized in working with artists and musicians. I knew when I met him at a Karma Moffitt concert that he was someone I would be willing to trust. He looked like a grandfather, a fact that rang some deeply hidden dark bell inside of me.

I was in therapy with him for several months before I encountered a wall. In my session, he had guided me into a hypnotherapy trance and we were exploring my childhood, when I literally came up against some kind of barrier in my psyche. I was frozen stiff. I couldn't move, see or remember anything. All I could tell him was that I had hit a wall. Indeed.

For years I had been aware of a wall around my heart keeping me from fully expressing my love, but I didn't know that it was quite literal in the psychological sense. Ken

acknowledged the wall's existence and I went home, nowhere left to go when the session ended. Terrified after that, I avoided sessions with him for nearly six months, becoming depressed and considering suicide on a daily basis.

Then one afternoon, tired of spending my days in bed curled in the fetal position, I got up to go to the bathroom, considering the idea of getting up and getting dressed, as well. As I walked around the tight little corner of the one room basement studio on my way there I passed the dark brown wall that held two of my small explorations into cunt paintings. (Oh, yeah, art saves lives!) While looking at them I suddenly thought "Grandfather Tash molested me!" I nearly fainted.

I had adored my G'pa and such a thought felt like utter blasphemy, but my body responded to it as truth. I remembered how I had avoided going to his funeral when he died; the creepy times, as I grew up, when he had come into the bathroom while I was taking a bath. I remembered how strongly I reacted when my brother told me how wonderful he was, knowing somehow it wasn't true. And, somehow just letting that thought in, as awful as it felt, suddenly freed me to move and consider other options besides suicide or immobility.

I returned to Ken and therapy. I stuck with

it until I had unraveled the psychological wall and could move forward. I was two years old when it all started. G'pa would take me out to the shed to keep him "company". Over the next several months he would have me lie on the work bench beside the window, take my clothes off, and insert a variety of tools into my vagina. Confused, I dissociated the fear and discomfort I felt with the spiders hanging in their webs in the window. I just couldn't associate it with my grandfather's behavior or the thick smear of his desire. It had to be the spiders, the dark, the old Chevy, the dust in the sunlight. My grandfather loved me.

Years later the dissociation and repressed memories I used to protect myself would result in accidents with tools. I didn't enjoy receiving oral sex until my fifties after years of therapy. Putting these words on paper, even now, causes me to feel dizzy and distant from my body, as if I were not quite here. But I am here and it is time to finish this narrative.

At three, my brother, Richard, was born. My mother and father left me, once again, in the care of my father's parents; my Tash grandparents. One morning while my G'ma visited in the front of the house with her sister, I was in the back bedroom where I slept when visiting them. The back bedroom was my sanctuary. I would sit in bed and daydream. It was my G'ma's realm;

her house, and safe. Not like the shed. But this particular morning grandfather came into the room. He grabbed me and started to take off my clothes. I resisted; telling him "No, this is grandma's house!" His reaction was volcanic. From my current vantage point as an adult I realize it was as if I had threatened his very existence. He picked me up from the bed and threw me face down on the floor. Shouting at the top of his lungs "You filthy little cunt!" he proceeded to stomp on the back of my neck. My grandmother and great aunt ran into the room shouting and stopped him from killing me.

It was summertime. It was hot in the backseat of the car where I lay strapped to a board to protect my already injured neck. The sun streaming in through the window terrified me as my grandmother and great aunt drove me to the hospital. Cool summers in San Francisco have helped take the edge off of the summer terrors that I have always felt since then. I remember the huge x-ray machine and the coldness of the table underneath as it loomed over me. The memory of the chafing of the plaster cast that went all the way up under my chin to protect my dislocated neck has left me with an abhorrence of ever having a double chin. And finally someone noticed my leg. "This child has had polio. Why hasn't she gotten treatment?" That began another saga. Embellished as the tale was told, that

I had been jumping on the bed and fell off and landed on my head dislocating my neck; another family cover up.

Seen through the eyes of a child, my grandfather's teachings on the annihilation of love seemed immutable.   I did everything in my power to protect my grandfather in my own memory, including disassociating my personality in order to repress the memory of the pain and fear. The experience of being molested and injured by a beloved adult, with an intention to kill me, translated into a belief that I was a flawed and unlovable being. Rarely have I allowed a man to enter my heart. When I have, because of those underlying beliefs, I've chosen unworthy men. Their behavior towards me confirmed those beliefs and protected my grandfather's memory. My grandfather's teaching seemed validated every time I've been disappointed in love.

It has taken me five years to finally finish these pages. Writing down these details allows me to finally reconcile the past with my present life. I can identify the lies and embrace the truth now that I no longer need to suppress the memories to protect my grandfather. It moves the trauma out of my body and locates it in the space of story. I can begin to envision a new future for myself. I no longer need to keep a wall around my heart to protect myself from the "annihilation of love" or choose men who are unworthy of my time and attention. I can learn to make considered choices, move slowly and allow myself to be in control of my responses in relationship rather than blindly jumping in feet first when someone is attracted to me. Even if I am inevitably hurt by others whom I love, I know I will not be annihilated because I have finally made peace with my past.

Deborah K. Tash
15AUG13
San Francisco, CA

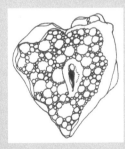

Changing The Order

Just now she woke up
Meditation still to come
Hearing the deep sigh
Precursor to orgasm
She changed the order

Reaching for the pleasure
Touching all those parts
Waiting in the folds
So rich with longing
To be stroked and entered

Finding the tools for self-love
Liquid for entry
Fantasies brimming over
While heartbeat and breath collide
Letting it take precedent for the day

07APR20

37

39

41

Continuum

As I prepare painted butterflies
Each one a prayer for expansion
To surround the ceramic cunt
Center piece of another act of reclaiming
I memorize the essential facet
My womanhood shared

The continuum of soul and sexuality
Manifest in butterflies and cunt
Those winged lovelies whose survival
Is as tenuous now as women's freedoms
Though we can raise our voices to declare
Write and make art to be heard

But butterflies who live their adult lives
Symbol of soul dedicated to their sexuality
Have only the voice of their beauty
As precious as women's sacred jewel
And we can raise our voices
To reclaim the Sacred Cunt for ourselves

10JUN19

44

Yes I Am!

How many times has your assertiveness
Been denigrated with
     You Cunt!
How many times have you been told to shut up
     You Cunt!

How many times have you heard a woman
Referred to in disgust
     You Cunt!
Because she was strong and had opinions
     You Cunt!

How many women hate their own cunts
Taught the jeweled beauty between their legs
Dirty! Smelly! Shameful!
Their pleasure palace as sinful
     You Cunt!

How many times 'til our wings are clipped
Heads bowed in submission
     You Cunt!
Are you still there?
     You Cunt!

Do you agree with those who have turned
Our sacred word of shared womanhood
     You Cunt!
Into the filthiest vile slander
     You Cunt!

Or are you ready to take a stand
To face them all and shout
     You Cunt!
Reclaiming at the top of your voice
     Yes I Am!

11JUN19

46

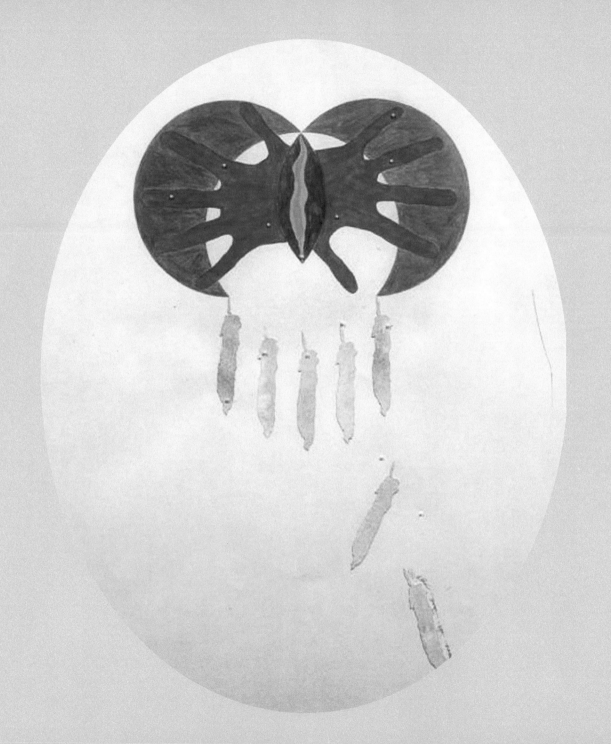

49

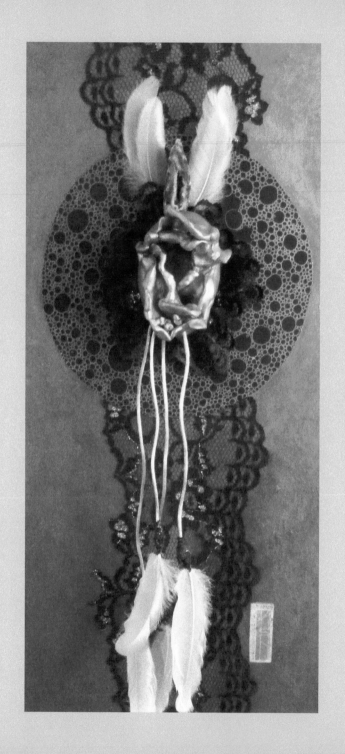

50

51

54

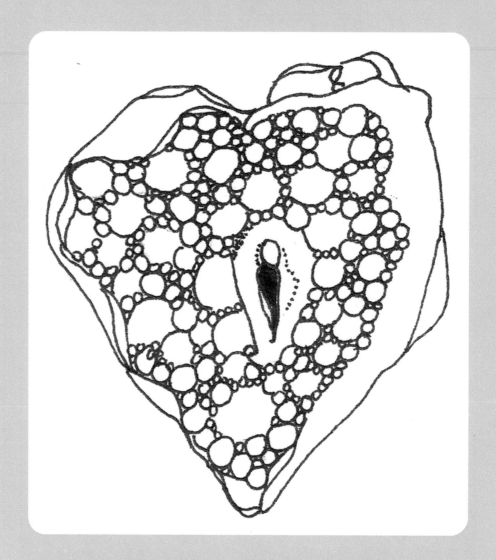

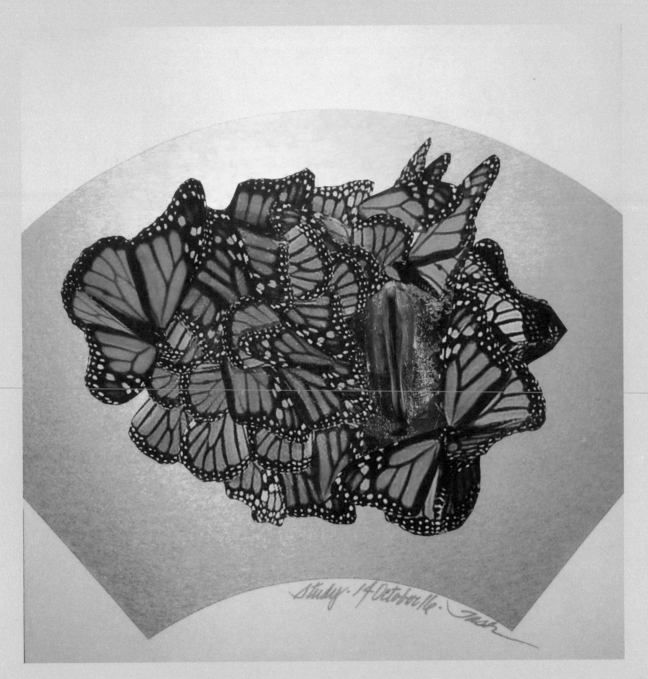

Study - 14 October 16 - Nash

60

TABLE OF IMAGES - I

TABLE OF IMAGES - II

Deborah K. Tash
White Wolf Woman
In Her Image Studio
inherimage@artlover.com
www.inherimagestudio.com

Photography:
Donnie Felton/Almac Camera
M. Joseph Schaller, PhD
Deborah K. Tash

Deborah Karen Tash, White Wolf Woman, a Shamanic Artist, award winning poet and healer, is currently Artist In Residence for herchurch and curator of ARISE GALLERY in San Francisco, California.

Creating as a spiritual practice and means of self-expression has been the foundation of her work both as a visual artist and poet. She combines both whimsy and Shamanic influence on the path of beauty in her art.

Working in series she allows idea, inspiration and dreams to guide her in the choices she makes determining the kinds of medium and techniques to employ for each piece.

She works with painting, mixed media, sculpture, mask, drawing, fiber, collage, photography and clay often weaving them together in a single multimedia expression as well as writing poetry.

Deborah continues to explore how to use symbol and image in order to uncover the shape and influence of transformation on her interior life and that of the viewer, as well.